Viola Time Joggers

a first book of very easy pieces for viola

Kathy and David Blackwell

Illustrations by

Martin Remphry

Welcome to the third edition of **Viola Time Joggers**. You'll find:

- open string pieces and tunes using the finger pattern 0–1–23–4
- duets—start with the staves marked ☆; come back and play the other part later!
- three new pieces, replacing nos. 3 and 29 and ensemble part no. 44
- audio play-along tracks available to download from www.oup.com/vtjoggers3e or to access on principal streaming platforms
- piano and viola accompaniments available separately in printed collections
- an ideal book to use alongside *Viola Time Starters*
- a book for viola that's also compatible with *Fiddle Time Joggers*

Teacher's note:

Forty-four of the 47 tunes from *Fiddle Time Joggers* are compatible with *Viola Time Joggers*. In a few pieces, some details are different between the two books, for example some bar numbers and introductions.

denotes a part that fits with *Fiddle Time Joggers*: these are printed in sequence in the book or on pages 32–5. In audio tracks 51–9, the part is played first by viola and piano, and then with the violin part added.

C string special denotes pieces that provide practice on the C string.

indicates the audio track number; it is given only where a piece number and its corresponding audio track number differ.

OXFORD
UNIVERSITY PRESS

OXFORD
UNIVERSITY PRESS

Great Clarendon Street, Oxford OX2 6DP, England

Oxford University Press is a department of the University of Oxford.
It furthers the University's aim of excellence in research, scholarship,
and education by publishing worldwide

Oxford is a registered trade mark of Oxford University Press
in the UK and in certain other countries

This collection © Oxford University Press 2005, 2013, and 2022

Kathy and David Blackwell have asserted their right under the Copyright, Designs
and Patents Act, 1988, to be identified as the Composers of this Work

Database right Oxford University Press (maker)

First published 2005. Reprinted with corrections 2013 and with amendments 2022

ISBN 978-0-19-356215-8

Music and text origination by Julia Bovee
Printed in Great Britain on acid-free paper by
Halstan & Co Ltd., Amersham, Bucks.

Contents

Open strings

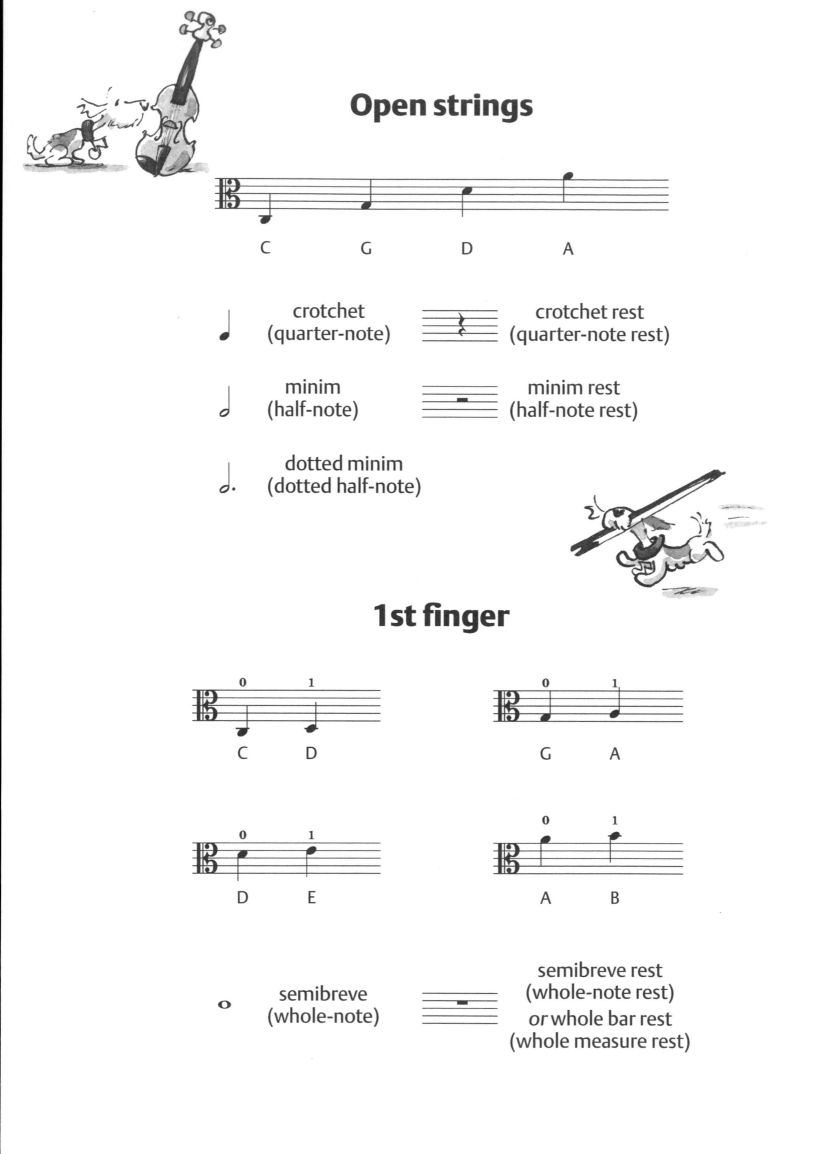

C   G   D   A

crotchet
(quarter-note)

crotchet rest
(quarter-note rest)

minim
(half-note)

minim rest
(half-note rest)

dotted minim
(dotted half-note)

1st finger

C   D

G   A

D   E

A   B

semibreve
(whole-note)

semibreve rest
(whole-note rest)
or whole bar rest
(whole measure rest)

1. Bow down, O Belinda

American folk tune

2. Under arrest!

KB & DB

Count 2 bars

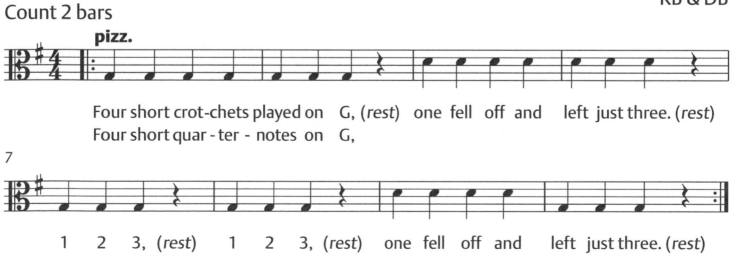

Four short crot-chets played on   G, (*rest*)   one fell   off and   left just three. (*rest*)
Four short quar - ter - notes on   G,

1   2   3, (*rest*)   1   2   3, (*rest*)   one fell   off and   left just three. (*rest*)

Say the word '*rest*' quietly to yourself as you play.

3. Someone plucks, someone bows

Traditional
Words KB & DB

Down, up goes the bow, when we're play - ing fast or slow;

Down, up goes the bow, when we're play - ing high or low.

48 🎧 🎻 **3. Someone plucks, someone bows**
(lower part of violin duit)

pizz.

4. Down up

C string special

KB & DB

arco

Down up A string, down up D string, down up G string, down up C string;

* Play the D and end with G.

* Fill in the letter names of these notes.

(No. 4 is not compatible with *Fiddle Time Joggers*.)

5. Two in a boat

American folk tune

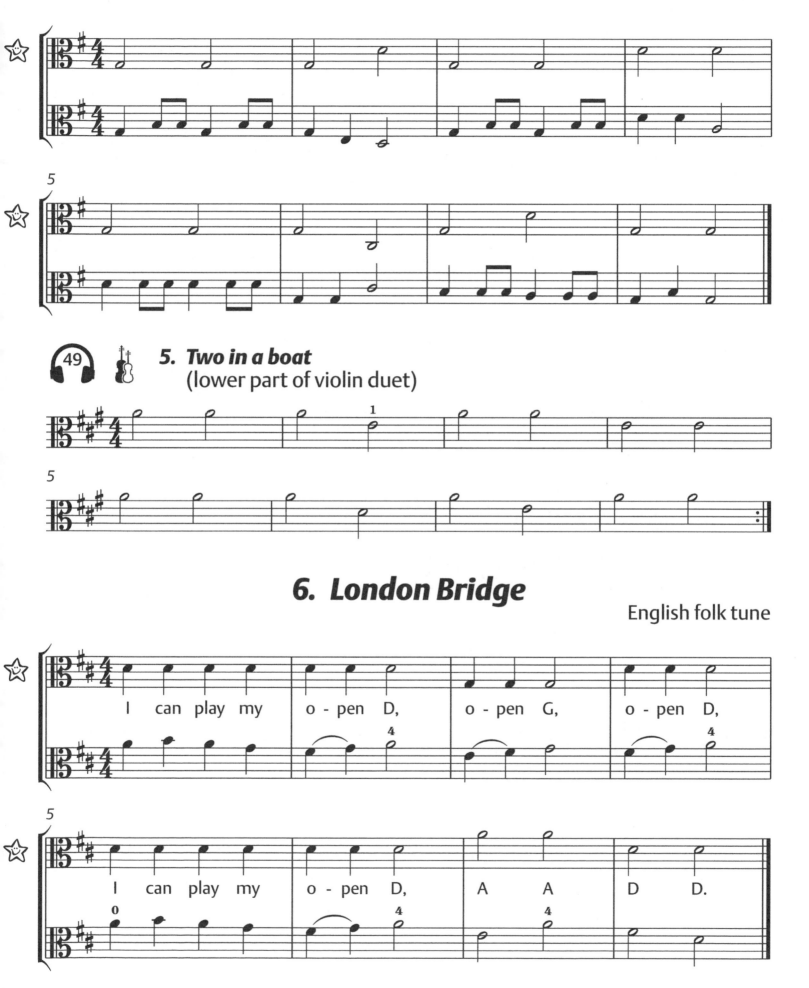

5. Two in a boat
(lower part of violin duet)

6. London Bridge

English folk tune

I can play my o-pen D, o-pen G, o-pen D,

I can play my o-pen D, A A D D.

7

7. Fast lane

KB & DB

Try even faster the second time through!

8. In flight

KB & DB

In the rests, let your bow make a circle as you swoop and soar like a bird.

9. Lift off!

KB & DB

Lift your bow off in each of the rests and let it orbit! (Make a circle with your right arm.)

Rhythm game:

Or - bit round the moon. (*etc.*)

10. Katie's waltz

Count 4 bars

KB & DB

11. Copy cat

KB & DB

Can you play what I play? D D E E

Fine

Can you play what I play? Play it now with me.

D.C. al Fine

Can you play what I play? A A B B

Can you play what I play? Play it now with me.

12. Tap dancer

KB & DB

* Hold the bow upright and tap the screw end of the bow on your music stand.

13. Rhythm fever

KB & DB

Count 2 bars

Rock tempo

Rhy-thm fe-ver, 1 2 3 4 feel the beat, 1 2 3 4

feel the rhy-thm, 1 2 3 4 in your feet. 1 2 3 4 Feel the rhy-thm

as you play it, feel the beat go 1 2 3 4 Rhy-thm fe-ver,

1 2 3 4 rhy-thm fe-ver, 1 2 3 4 rhy-thm fe-ver, oh yeah!

14. Here it comes!

(adapted melody)

KB & DB

Through the teeth and past the gums, so watch out, tum-my, here it comes!

Through the teeth and past the gums, so watch out, tum-my, here it comes!

* Think of a foody rhythm and play it on these notes.

Here is an idea to start you off:

Fish and chips and ice cream.

15. So there!

(adapted melody)

KB & DB

Count 4 bars

Brightly

So there!

16. Rowing boat

KB & DB

Gently

Getting slower

17. Ally bally

Scottish folk tune

17. Ally bally
(lower part of violin duet)

18. Tiptoe, boo!

KB & DB

Spookily!

Tip-toe tip-toe   tip-toe, boo! (*etc.*)

Boo!
(shout!)

Also try playing this pizzicato.

19. Travellin' slow

KB & DB

In first gear

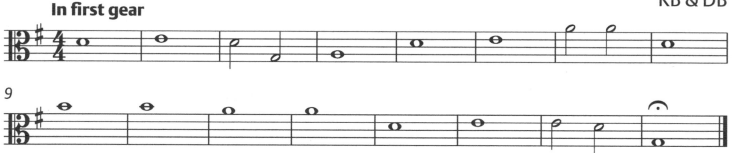

20. C string boogie

C string special

KB & DB

With a gentle swing
pizz.

* Turn around or, if you are sitting, stand up and sit down again!

20. Lazy cowboy—see page 32.

2nd finger

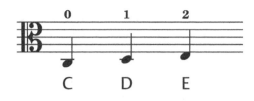

C   D   E

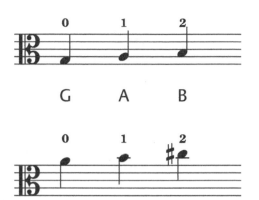

G   A   B

D   E   F#

A   B   C#

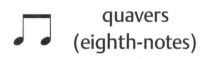 quavers
(eighth-notes)

21. Off to Paris

French folk tune

22. Clare's song

KB & DB

23. City lights

KB & DB

24. Daydream

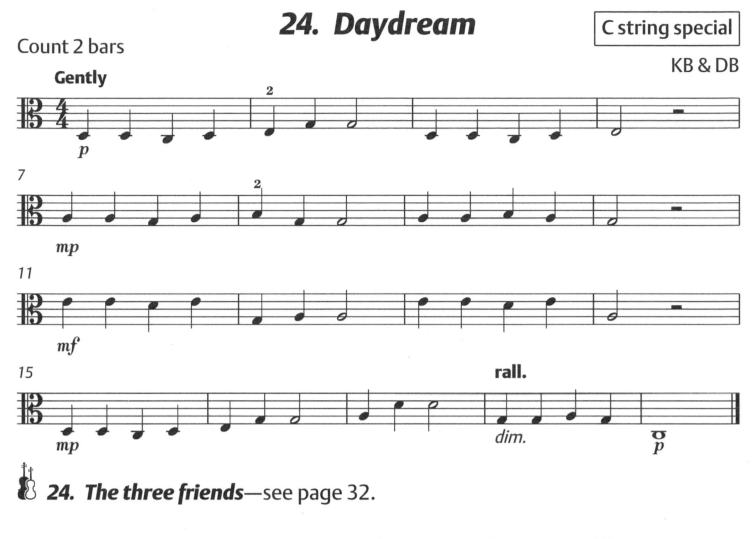

Count 2 bars

Gently

24. The three friends—see page 32.

C string special

KB & DB

25. On the prowl

C string special

KB & DB

With menace

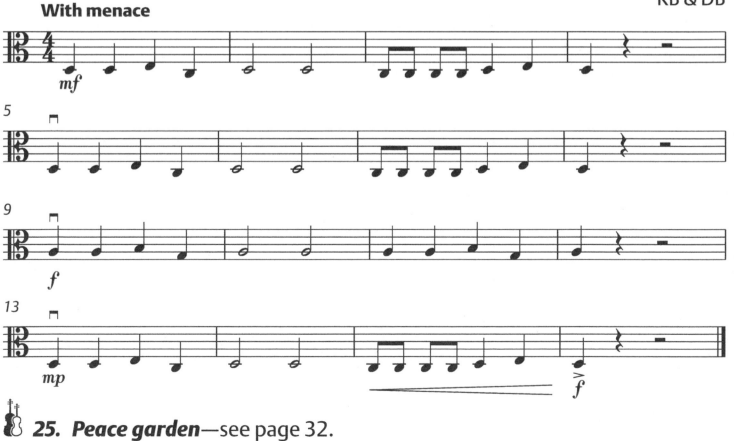

25. Peace garden—see page 32.

26. Summer sun

KB & DB

From now on, you'll be able to play both parts of the duets.

27. Phoebe in her petticoat

American folk tune

Swap parts when you do the repeat.

28. Ready, steady, go now!

(adapted melody)

KB & DB

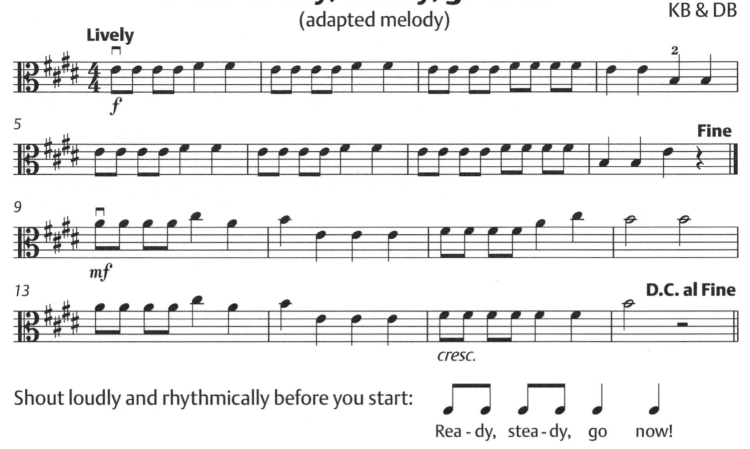

Shout loudly and rhythmically before you start:

Rea - dy, stea - dy, go now!

29. Cooking in the kitchen

KB & DB

30. Happy go lucky (for Iain)

Count 4 bars

KB & DB

Sunnily

31. The mocking bird

American folk tune

Now you can play the harder part of 'Someone plucks, someone bows' on page 6.

3rd and 4th fingers

32. Algy met a bear

KB & DB
Words anon.

mf

Al - gy met a bear, a bear met Al - gy. The

mf

bear was bul - gy, the bulge was Al - gy!

slur

Swap parts when you do the repeat.

33. Listen to the rhythm

Count 4 bars

KB & DB

Lis - ten to the rhy-thm on my vi - o - la.
Crot-chets sound like
Quar - ter - notes like

this:
this:
Crot-chets sound like   that!
Quar - ter - notes like   that!

Lis - ten to the rhy-thm on my vi - o - la.
Mi - nims sound like
Half-notes sound like

this:
this:
Mi - nims sound like   that!
Half-notes sound like   that!

Lis - ten to the rhy-thm on my vi - o - la.
Se - mi - breves like
Whole-notes sound like

this:
this:
Se - mi - breves like   that!
Whole-notes sound like   that!

23

34. Cattle ranch blues

KB & DB

Stompy

mf

5

cresc.

9

rit.

f

35. In the groove

Count 2 bars

KB & DB

Swing

mf cresc.

7

f

11

mf cresc.

15

f

20

rit.

mp

Now go back to page 15 and play the harder part of 'Off to Paris'.

35. In the groove—see page 33.

36. Stamping dance

Czech folk tune

Try the harder part of 'Bow down, O Belinda' on page 5.

37. Distant bells

Count 2 bars

KB & DB

Now go back to page 16 and play 'Clare's song', slurring three crotchets (quarter-notes) to a bow.

38. Lazy scale

KB & DB

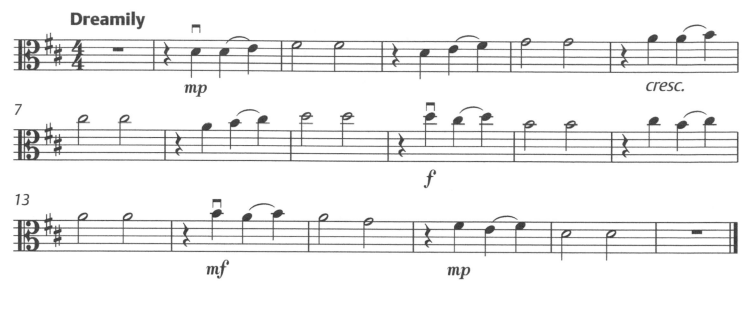

39. Runaway train

C string special

KB & DB

Count 4 bars

 **39. The old castle**—see page 33.

40. Rocking horse

Count 4 bars

KB & DB

41. Patrick's reel

Count 2 bars

KB & DB

42. Calypso time

Count 2 bars

KB & DB

Now go back to page 13 and play the harder part of 'Ally bally'.

42. Calypso time—see page 34.

43. Tudor tune

C string special

KB & DB

44. Chopsticks for two

C string special

KB & DB

Chunky

Now try the harder part of 'Copy cat' on page 10.

44. Rocky mountain—see page 34.

45. Carrion crow

American folk tune

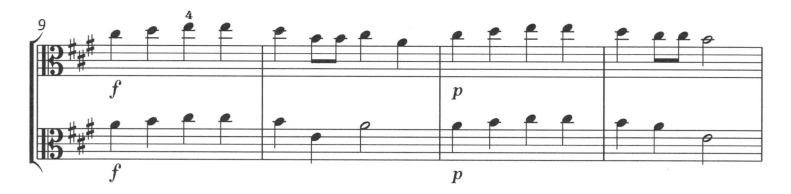

Try the harder part of 'Two in a boat' and 'London Bridge' on page 7.

45. Carrion crow—see page 35.

46. Flying high

KB & DB

Smoothly

mp

mf

rit.

f   *mp*

p

(No. 46 is not compatible with *Fiddle Time Joggers*.)

47. Viola Time

Count 4 bars

KB & DB

Easy going

𝄋 **(a tempo)**

f

1.

2.

pizz. Fine

mp

rit.   **D.𝄋 al Fine**

cresc.   *mf*

🎻 **47. Fiddle Time**—see page 35.

31

🎻 Ensemble parts

These additional parts are compatible with, and are numbered as, the pieces in *Fiddle Time Joggers.*

20. Lazy cowboy
(ensemble part)

KB & DB

24. The three friends
(ensemble part for violin duet)

Finnish folk tune

25. Peace garden
(adapted melody)

KB & DB

35. In the groove

(ensemble part)

KB & DB

39. The old castle

(ensemble part)

KB & DB

42. Calypso time
(ensemble part)

KB & DB

Say this rhythm before you start to play:

Let's play Ca - lyp - so

44. Rocky mountain
(lower part of violin duet)

American folk tune

45. Carrion crow
(ensemble part for violin duet)

American folk tune

47. Fiddle Time
(ensemble part)

KB & DB

Count 4 bars

Music Fact-Finder Page

Here are some of the words and signs you will find in some of your pieces!

How to play it

pizzicato or pizz. = pluck
arco = with the bow
⊓ = down bow
V = up bow
> = accent
𝄎 = tremolo

Don't get lost!

‖: :‖ = repeat marks

┌1.┐ ┌2.┐ = first and second time bars
D.C. al Fine = repeat from the beginning and stop at **Fine**
D.𝄋 al Fine = repeat from the sign 𝄋 and stop at **Fine**
rit. = gradually getting slower
a tempo = back to the first speed
⌢ = pause

Volume control

p (*piano*) = quiet
mp (*mezzo-piano*) = moderately quiet
mf (*mezzo-forte*) = moderately loud
f (*forte*) = loud
ff (*fortissimo*) = very loud
⎯⎯⎯⎯⎯⎯ or *crescendo* (*cresc.*) = getting gradually louder
⎯⎯⎯⎯⎯⎯ or *diminuendo* (*dim.*) = getting gradually quieter